Sunshine

Pupil's Book 1

Class 3

Cornelsen

Contents

Getting started		3
Unit 1	Meeting friends	4
Unit 2	Pets in the garden	6
Unit 3	At school	10
Unit 4	The second-hand shop	14
Unit 5	Free-time activities	18
Unit 6	In the park	22
Unit 7	Special days	26
Word list		30

Symbols

CD 1.8 listen to the CD · CD 1 track 8

read

listen

play

speak

That's English

1 Read the words. Find the pictures: computer, cowboy, mountain bike, skateboard.

2 Find more English words in the picture.

In the street

1 Listen. Point to the numbers.

2 Listen. What number is Harry's house?

CD 1.9

Landeskundliche Informationen erfahren (S. 65) · einen Hörtext verstehen (S. 67)

Hopscotch

CD 1.8

1 **Listen and point.**

2 **Say the numbers.**

3 **Play hopscotch.**

Dialogue: Favourite colours

1 **Read the dialogue.**

2 **Talk to a partner.**

A phone call on Sunday morning

CD 1.16

1 Listen. Who's calling Harry?

Dialogue: A phone call

1 Read the dialogue.

2 Talk to a partner.

Einen Hörtext verstehen (S. 83) · einen Dialog sprechen (S. 84)

In the garden shed

1 Look at the picture. What pets are there in the garden shed?

2 Listen. What are the children's pets?

CD 1.19

Story: Rabbit's party

1 Read the story.

2 Act it out.

Eine Geschichte lesen (S. 91) · eine Geschichte nachspielen (S. 91)

Board game: The garden race

1 Play the game.

3 At school

A day at school

1 **Look at the the pictures. Talk about the pictures.**

CD 1.27

2 **Listen. Point to the pictures.**

3 **Read.**

1

a school bus

2

3

playing hopscotch

Landeskundliche Informationen verstehen (S. 101) · einen Hörtext verstehen (S. 101)

4

6

7

lunch at school

Story: Jack's bad day

CD 1.30

1 Listen to the story.

2 Read the story.

Eine Geschichte verstehen und selber lesen (S. 108)

Game: Take five

1 Read the text.

2 Play the game in groups of four.

(1) Take five cards from each pupil's word box:

(2) Put all the cards together.

(3) Shuffle the 20 cards.

(4) Give five cards to each child.

(5) Ask the questions.

4 The second-hand shop

At the second-hand shop

1 Look at the shop. Talk about the shop.

2 Read the words. Find the pictures.

jacket

Wortschatz und Redemittel üben (S. 119) · Wortschatz und Redemittel festigen (S. 121)

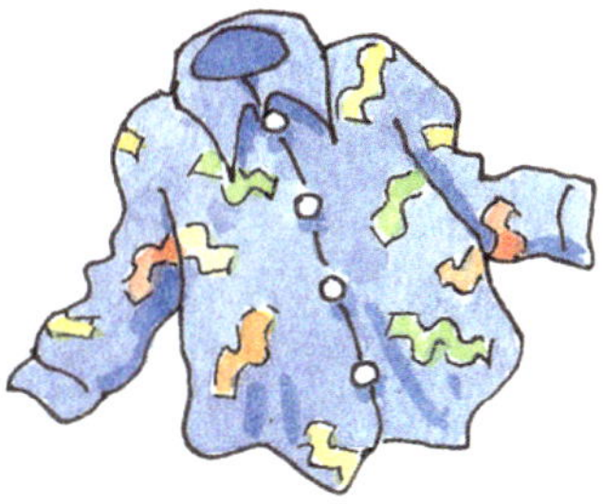

shirt

dress

hat

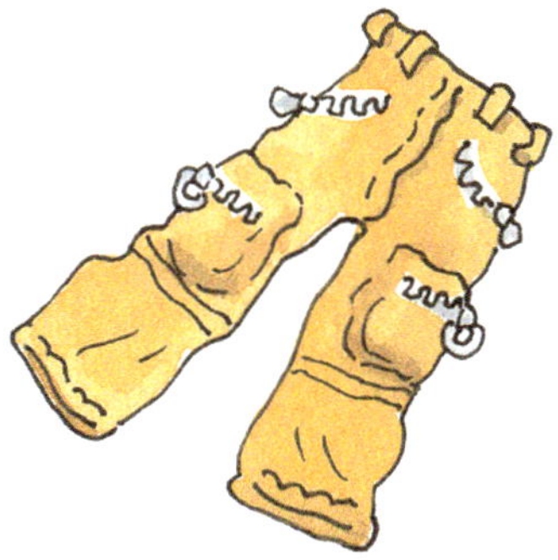

trousers

pullover

gloves

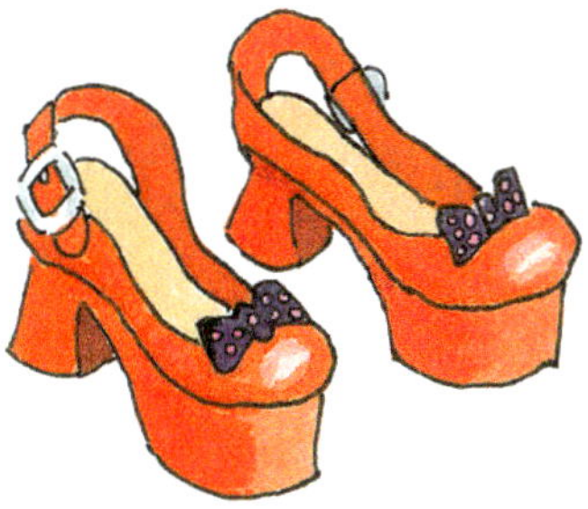

shoes

skirt

Dialogue: Clothes

1 Read the dialogue.

2 Talk to a partner.

Story: A funny boy

1 Look at the pictures. Talk about the pictures.

2 Read the story.

5 Free-time activities

Song: What do you like?

CD 2.3

1 Listen to the song. Point to the pictures.

2 Sing the song.

Ein Lied singen (S. 135, 137)

Dialogue: Free-time activities

1 **Read the dialogue.**

2 **Talk to a partner.**

Rhyme: Where's the cat?

CD 2.7

1 **Listen to the rhyme. Point to the pictures.**

2 **Read the rhyme.**

Where's the cat? Where's the cat?
Is she in the living room – watching TV?
Is she in the kitchen – drinking my tea?

Where's the cat? Where's the cat?
Is she in the bedroom – eating my shoe?
Is she in the bathroom – playing with shampoo?

Where's the cat? Where's the cat?
There she is – sleeping in Mum's favourite hat.

Spot the difference

1 **Look at the pictures. Where's Harry in house number 1? Where's Harry in house number 2?**

1

2

Aussagen zu Bildern treffen: Wortschatz festigen (S. 146)

Story: The babysitters

CD 2.8

1 Listen. Point to the right pictures.

2 Read the story.

CD 2.8

3 Listen again. What picture is in the story?

A day in the park

1 Look at the picture. Talk about the picture.

2 Find the numbers. Say: Number 10 is on ...

Wortschatz einführen (S. 153)

Rhyme: I eat apples

CD 2.13

1 **Listen to the rhyme.**

2 **Look at the pictures. Point to the right pictures.**

3 **Read the rhyme.**

I eat apples – crunch, crunch, crunch.
I eat peaches – munch, munch, munch.
I eat oranges – lick, lick, lick.
I eat ice cream – quick, quick, quick.

I eat strawberries – chew, chew, chew.
I eat lemons – eww, eww, eww.
I eat cherries – click, click, click.
I eat ice cream – quick, quick, quick.

At the kiosk

1 Talk about the picture. How much is an orange juice? How much are the peanuts?

CD 2.15

2 Listen. Which ice cream does the boy want?

Dialogue: Buying ice cream

1 Read the dialogue.

2 Talk to a partner.

Redemittel einführen (S. 159)
Einen Hörtext verstehen (S. 161) · einen Dialog lesen und sprechen (S. 161)

Story: Where's my ice cream?

CD 2.16

1 Listen to the story.

2 Read the story. Is it right or wrong?

7 Special days

Birthdays

CD 2.18

1 Listen to the song.

2 Talk about the picture.

3 Sing the song.

Birthday song

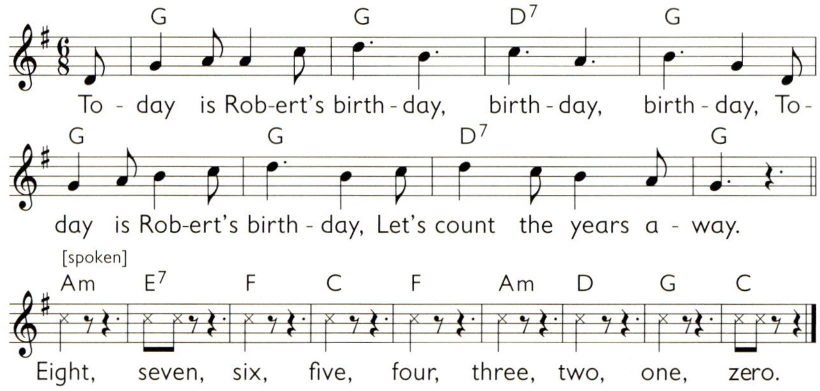

Halloween

1 Talk about the picture. Count the ghosts, monsters, pumpkins, skeletons, …

2 Listen to the rhymes.

CD 2.21

3 Read the rhymes.

Trick or treat,
Listen to the beat.
We want only
Sweets to eat.

Trick or treat,
Smell my feet.
Give me something
Good to eat!

Christmas

1 Look at the pictures. Talk about the pictures.

2 Listen and point.

Landeskundliche Informationen erfahren, Wortschatz üben (S. 179)

Easter

1 Talk about the picture.

2 Listen to the song.

CD 2.25

3 Sing the song.

Word list

A
apple Apfel

B
banana Banane
bedroom Schlafzimmer
big groß
birthday Geburtstag
birthday cake Geburtstagskuchen
birthday card Geburtstagskarte
birthday present Geburtstagsgeschenk
blue blau
book Buch
boring langweilig

C
can können
carrot Möhre
cat Katze
cherry Kirsche
chocolate Schokolade
Christmas Weihnachten
Christmas Day Weihnachtstag (25.12.)
Christmas Eve Heiligabend (24.12.)
Christmas tree Weihnachtsbaum
colour Farbe
colour ausmalen
come kommen
cowboy Cowboy

D
dog Hund
draw zeichnen
dress Kleid
drink Getränk
drink trinken

E
Easter Ostern
Easter basket Osterkorb
Easter bunny Osterhase
Easter egg Osterei
eat essen
eight acht
eighty achtzig

F
Father Christmas Weihnachtsmann
favourite Lieblings-
felt tip Filzstift
fifty fünfzig
five fünf
food Essen
football Fußball
forty vierzig
four vier

G
garden shed Gartenhaus
ghost Gespenst
gloves Handschuhe
glue stick Klebstift
green grün
guinea pig Meerschweinchen

H

hamster Hamster
hat Mütze
here hier
house Haus

I

ice cream Eiscreme
in-line skates Inlineskates

J

jacket Jacke
juice Saft

L

lemon Zitrone
lettuce Salat
like mögen
listening to music Musik hören
living room Wohnzimmer
lunch Mittagessen
lunch box Brotdose

M

meeting friends Freunde treffen
milk Milch
monster Monster
mountain bike Mountainbike

N

nine neun
ninety neunzig
number Nummer, Zahl

O

on auf
one eins
orange orange
orange Apfelsine
orange juice Orangensaft

P

peach Pfirsich
peanuts Erdnüsse
pen Füller
pencil Bleistift
pencil case Federmappe
pencil sharpener Bleistiftspitzer
pet Haustier
pink rosa
play spielen
playing computer games Computerspiele spielen
playing football Fußball spielen
popcorn Popcorn
pullover Pullover
pumpkin Kürbis

R

rabbit Kaninchen
rat Ratte
read lesen
red rot
reindeer Rentier
rubber Radiergummi
ruler Lineal

S

school Schule
school bag Schultasche
school bus Schulbus
scissors Schere
scooter Roller

seven sieben
seventy siebzig
shirt Hemd
shoes Schuhe
shop Laden
six sechs
sixty sechzig
skateboard Skateboard
skeleton Skelett
skirt Rock
spider Spinne
stocking Strumpf
strawberry Erdbeere

T

ten zehn
thirty dreißig
three drei
trousers Hose
twenty zwanzig
two zwei

W

watching TV fernsehen
witch Hexe

Y

yellow gelb